REFLECTIONS
FOR
LENT 2023

REFLECTIONS
FOR
LENT

22 February – 8 April 2023

KATE BRUCE
GRAHAM JAMES
MARK OAKLEY

with Holy Week reflections by
PAULA GOODER

Church House Publishing
Church House
Great Smith Street
London SW1P 3AZ

ISBN 978 1 78140 304 4

Published 2022 by Church House Publishing
Copyright © The Archbishops' Council 2022

The opinions expressed in this book are those of the
authors and do not necessarily reflect the official policy of
the General Synod or The Archbishops' Council of the
Church of England.

Liturgical editor: Peter Moger
Series editor: Hugh Hillyard-Parker
Designed and typeset by Hugh Hillyard-Parker
Copyedited by Ros Connelly
Printed by CPI Group (UK) Ltd, Croydon CR0 4YY

What do you think of *Reflections for Lent*?

We'd love to hear from you – simply email us at

publishing@churchofengland.org

or write to us at

Church House Publishing, Church House,
Great Smith Street, London SW1P 3AZ.

Visit **www.dailyprayer.org.uk** for more
information on the *Reflections* series, ordering
and subscriptions.

Contents

About the authors vi

About *Reflections for Lent* 1

Lent – jousting within the self 2
MARK OAKLEY

Building daily prayer into daily life 4
RACHEL TREWEEK

Lectio Divina – a way of reading the Bible 6
STEPHEN COTTRELL

Wednesday 22 February to Saturday 4 March 8
KATE BRUCE

Monday 6 March to Saturday 18 March 18
MARK OAKLEY

Monday 20 March to Saturday 1 April 30
GRAHAM JAMES

HOLY WEEK
Monday 3 April to Saturday 8 April 42
PAULA GOODER

Morning Prayer – a simple form 48

Seasonal Prayers of Thanksgiving 50

The Lord's Prayer and The Grace 51

An Order for Night Prayer (Compline) 52

About the authors

Kate Bruce is a serving RAF Chaplain. She writes in the area of homiletics, and has published a number of books and articles in this field. She offers day conferences in preaching around the country, and preaches regularly in a variety of contexts. She enjoys running, and writes and performs stand-up comedy in her spare time. She is Visiting Fellow at St John's College, Durham.

Stephen Cottrell is the Archbishop of York, having previously been Bishop of Chelmsford. He is a well-known writer and speaker on evangelism, spirituality and catechesis. He is one of the team that produced *Pilgrim*, the popular course for the Christian Journey.

Paula Gooder is Chancellor of St Paul's Cathedral, London. She is a writer and lecturer in biblical studies, author of a number of books including *Women of Holy Week; Journalling the Psalms; The Parables* and *Phoebe: A Story*, and a co-author of the Pilgrim course. She is also a Licensed Lay Minister (Reader) in the Church of England.

Graham James was Bishop of Norwich for almost 20 years until his retirement in 2019. Since then he has chaired the Paterson Inquiry, an independent inquiry for the Government on patient safety in the NHS and private healthcare. Earlier in his ministry he was Bishop of St Germans in his native Cornwall and Chaplain to two Archbishops of Canterbury. He has now returned to Cornwall where he ministers as an honorary assistant bishop. More widely, he has recently been appointed to the Human Fertilization & Embryology Authority.

Mark Oakley is Dean and Fellow of St John's College, Cambridge, and Honorary Canon Theologian of Wakefield Cathedral in the Diocese of Leeds. He is the author of *The Collage of God* (2001), *The Splash of Words: Believing in Poetry* (2016), and *My Sour Sweet Days: George Herbert and the Journey of the Soul* (2019) as well as articles and reviews, in the areas of faith, poetry, human rights and literature. He is Visiting Lecturer in the department of Theology and Religious Studies at King's College London.

Rachel Treweek is Bishop of Gloucester and the first female diocesan bishop in England. She served in two parishes in London and was Archdeacon of Northolt and later Hackney. Prior to ordination she was a speech and language therapist and is a trained practitioner in conflict transformation.

About *Reflections for Lent*

Based on the *Common Worship Lectionary* readings for Morning Prayer, these daily reflections are designed to refresh and inspire times of personal prayer. The aim is to provide rich, contemporary and engaging insights into Scripture.

Each page lists the lectionary readings for the day, with the main psalms for that day highlighted in **bold**. The collect of the day – either the *Common Worship* collect or the shorter additional collect – is also included.

For those using this book in conjunction with a service of Morning Prayer, the following conventions apply: a psalm printed in parentheses is omitted if it has been used as the opening canticle at that office; a psalm marked with an asterisk may be shortened if desired.

A short reflection is provided on either the Old or New Testament reading. Popular writers, experienced ministers, biblical scholars and theologians contribute to this series, all bringing their own emphases, enthusiasms and approaches to biblical interpretation.

Regular users of Morning Prayer and *Time to Pray* (from *Common Worship: Daily Prayer*) and anyone who follows the Lectionary for their regular Bible reading will benefit from the rich variety of traditions represented in these stimulating and accessible pieces.

The book also includes both a simple form of Common Worship: Morning Prayer (see pages 48–49) and a short form of Night Prayer, also known as Compline (see pages 52–55), particularly for the benefit of those readers who are new to the habit of the Daily Office or for any reader while travelling.

Lent – jousting within the self

It has been said that the heart of the human problem is the problem of the human heart. Lent is time set aside each year to take this thought seriously.

A few years ago, there was a story in the papers about a painting by Pieter Bruegel the Elder. It is currently on display in Vienna's marvellous Kunsthistorisches Museum, but Krakow's National Museum claims it is theirs and that it was stolen by the wife of the city's Nazi governor in 1939 during the occupation of Poland.

The painting is called 'The Fight Between Carnival and Lent' and it was painted in 1559. It is a beautifully typical Bruegel painting. It is a large, crowded canvas with nearly 200 men, women and children depicted on it. We find ourselves looking down on a town square during a riotous festival. The painting can be looked at in two halves. On the right, we see a church with people leaving after prayer. We see them giving alms to the poor, feeding the hungry, helping those with disability, calling attention to their need and tending to the dying. On the left, we see an inn. Congregated around it are beer drinkers, gamblers, various saucy types. The vulnerable nearby are not noticed, including a solitary procession of lepers. Instead, a man vomits out of a window and another bangs his head against a wall.

In the foreground, we see two figures being pulled towards each other on floats. One is Lady Lent, gaunt and unshowy, dressed as a nun, with followers eating pretzels and fish as well as drawing fresh water from a large well. The other is Carnival, a fat figure, armed with a meat spit and a pork pie helmet. He's followed by masked carousers. A man in yellow – the symbolic colour of deceit – pushes his float, though he looks rather weighed down by cups and a bag of belongings. In the background, we see, on the left, some stark, leafless trees, but on the right side, buds are awakening on the branches and, as if to see them better, a woman is busily cleaning her windows.

It is an allegorical delight, and we might do worse than take a close look at it sometime this Lent. It's tempting to classify each human there as either good or bad, secular or faithful, kind or indifferent. We love to place people into convenient cutlery trays, dividing us all up as is most useful for us. What I love about this painting, however, is that it reminds me that we are all similarly made with two halves.

For so many of us, there is a constant fight going on within between the times we are negligent and the times we are careful; days in which we get through with a self that enjoys its own attention, being centre-stage, and days when our self just feels somehow more itself when not being selfish. I have an impulse to pray; I have an impulse to avoid or forget it. There are parts of me grotesquely masked, and there are parts of me trying to clean my windows on a ladder, as it were, wanting to increase transparency and attention to the world, to me and to my relationships.

Lent begins with a small dusty cross being made on my head, the hard case that protects the organ that makes decisions. The season starts by asking me to imagine how life might be if the imprint of Christ's courageous compassion might make itself felt and acted on, rather than just passionately talked about. Lent knows what we are like. It has seen the painting. It has read a bit of Freud, some history books, political manifestos and memoirs of hurt and achievement. It winces at our cyclical, self-destructive repetitions. It believes in us, though, knowing that, with God and each other, if we reach outside of our own hardened little worlds, we set the scene to be helped and, maybe, even changed. That would be good – for me and those who live with me.

In the Gospels, the 40 days Jesus spent in the beguiling wilderness immediately followed his baptism. Coming up out of the water, he had heard the unmistakable voice that matters, telling him he was cherished, wanted and ready. He then goes into the heat spending time with himself, hearing other voices that want him to live down to them; but he knows that his vocation can only be lived when he learns to live up to the one voice he heard that day in the river, not down to the ones that want him to live some conventionally indifferent and submerged existence as a consumer of the world and not as a citizen of the kingdom. We follow him. Where he goes, so do we. A wilderness Lent is needed more than ever to do some heart-repair and start becoming Christians again.

I don't know who owns the Bruegel painting. What I do know is that its themes belong to all of us; our inner landscape matches his rowdy town square. As long as the fight continues, the soul will be alive.

Mark Oakley

Building daily prayer into daily life

In our morning routines there are many tasks we do without giving much thought to them, and others that we do with careful attention. Daily prayer and Bible reading is a strange mixture of these. These are disciplines (and gifts) that we as Christians should have in our daily pattern, but they are not tasks to be ticked off. Rather they are a key component of our developing relationship with God. In them is *life* – for the fruits of this time are to be lived out by us – and to be most fruitful, the task requires both purpose and letting go.

In saying a daily office of prayer, we make a deliberate decision to spend time with God – the God who is always with us. In prayer and attentive reading of the Scriptures, there is both a conscious entering into God's presence and a 'letting go' of all we strive to control: both are our acknowledgement that it is God who is God.

> *… come before his presence with a song…*
>
> *Know that the Lord is God;*
> *it is he that has made us and we are his;*
> *we are his people and the sheep of his pasture.*
>
> *Enter his gates with thanksgiving…*
>
> *(Psalm 100, a traditional Canticle at Morning Prayer)*

If we want a relationship with someone to deepen and grow, we need to spend time with that person. It can be no surprise that the same is true between us and God.

In our daily routines, I suspect that most of us intentionally look in the mirror; occasionally we might see beyond the surface of our external reflection and catch a glimpse of who we truly are. For me, a regular pattern of daily prayer and Bible reading is like a hard look in a clean mirror: it gives a clear reflection of myself, my life and the world in which I live. But it is more than that, for in it I can also see the reflection of God who is most clearly revealed in Jesus Christ and present with us now in the Holy Spirit.

This commitment to daily prayer is about our relationship with the God who is love. St Paul, in his great passage about love, speaks of now seeing 'in a mirror, dimly' but one day seeing face to face: 'Now I know only in part; then I will know fully, even as I have been fully known' (1 Corinthians 13.12). Our daily prayer is part of that seeing in a mirror dimly, and it is also part of our deep yearning for an ever-clearer vision of our God. As we read Scripture, the past and the future converge in the present moment. We hear words from long ago – some of which can appear strange and confusing – and yet, the Holy Spirit is living and active in the present. In this place of relationship and revelation, we open ourselves to the possibility of being changed, of being reshaped in a way that is good for us and all creation.

It is important that the words of prayer and scripture should penetrate deep within rather than be a mere veneer. A quiet location is therefore a helpful starting point. For some, domestic circumstances or daily schedule make that difficult, but it is never impossible to become more fully present to God. The depths of our being can still be accessed no matter the world's clamour and activity. An awareness of this is all part of our journey from a false sense of control to a place of letting go, to a place where there is an opportunity for transformation.

Sometimes in our attention to Scripture there will be connection with places of joy or pain; we might be encouraged or provoked or both. As we look and see and encounter God more deeply, there will be thanksgiving and repentance; the cries of our heart will surface as we acknowledge our needs and desires for ourselves and the world. The liturgy of Morning Prayer gives this voice and space.

I find it helpful to begin Morning Prayer by lighting a candle. This marks my sense of purpose and my acknowledgement of Christ's presence with me. It is also a silent prayer for illumination as I prepare to be attentive to what I see in the mirror, both of myself and of God. Amid the revelation of Scripture and the cries of my heart, the constancy of the tiny flame bears witness to the hope and light of Christ in all that is and will be.

When the candle is extinguished, I try to be still as I watch the smoke disappear. For me, it is symbolic of my prayers merging with the day. I know that my prayer and the reading of Scripture are not the smoke and mirrors of delusion. Rather, they are about encounter and discovery as I seek to venture into the day to love and serve the Lord as a disciple of Jesus Christ.

+ Rachel Treweek

Lectio Divina – a way of reading the Bible

Lectio Divina is a contemplative way of reading the Bible. It dates back to the early centuries of the Christian Church and was established as a monastic practice by Benedict in the sixth century. It is a way of praying the Scriptures that leads us deeper into God's word. We slow down. We read a short passage more than once. We chew it over slowly and carefully. We savour it. Scripture begins to speak to us in a new way. It speaks to us personally, and aids that union we have with God through Christ, who is himself the Living Word.

Make sure you are sitting comfortably. Breathe slowly and deeply. Ask God to speak to you through the passage that you are about to read.

This way of praying starts with our silence. We often make the mistake of thinking prayer is about what we say to God. It is actually the other way round. God wants to speak to us. He will do this through the Scriptures. So don't worry about what to say. Don't worry if nothing jumps out at you at first. God is patient. He will wait for the opportunity to get in. He will give you a word and lead you to understand its meaning for you today.

First reading: Listen

As you read the passage listen for a word or phrase that attracts you. Allow it to arise from the passage as if it is God's word for you today. Sit in silence repeating the word or phrase in your head.

Then say the word or phrase aloud.

Second reading: Ponder

As you read the passage again, ask how this word or phrase speaks to your life and why it has connected with you. Ponder it carefully. Don't worry if you get distracted – it may be part of your response to offer to God. Sit in silence and then frame a single sentence that begins to say aloud what this word or phrase says to you.

Third reading: Pray

As you read the passage for the last time, ask what Christ is calling from you. What is it that you need to do or consider or relinquish or take on as a result of what God is saying to you in this word or phrase? In the silence that follows the reading, pray for the grace of the Spirit to plant this word in your heart.

If you are in a group, talk for a few minutes and pray with each other.

If you are on your own, speak your prayer to God either aloud or in the silence of your heart.

If there is time, you may even want to read the passage a fourth time, and then end with the same silence before God with which you began.

++Stephen Cottrell

Wednesday 22 February
Ash Wednesday

Psalm **38**
Daniel 9.3-6, 17-19
1 Timothy 6.6-19

1 Timothy 6.6-19

'... command them not ... to set their hopes on the uncertainty of riches, but rather on God who richly provides' (v.17)

Jeremiah takes aim at the people's attempts at self-reliance through the metaphor of digging cisterns. A futile example of cistern digging is accumulating riches believing this will bring peace and happiness. Money is neutral, but 'the love of money is a root of all kinds of evil'. It breeds self-reliance, airbrushing out the truth of our dependence on God for each breath and every heartbeat. When we fall for self-reliance, we become trapped in the need to grasp, hoard and stockpile. We become defensive, suspicious and manacled to the myth of scarcity. Generosity withers. Community founders. Individualism runs rampant.

Ash Wednesday urges us to put down the spade and examine our own cistern-digging habits. Is it cash in the attic and money in the bank that helps us sleep at night? Foolishness. We 'brought nothing into the world, so that we can take nothing out', except our relationship with God. Invest here.

God 'richly provides us with everything for our enjoyment'. There is no need to grasp and accrue and hoard. But how easily we forget. How easily we mistrust and think we'd better have an insurance policy. How readily we forfeit the freedom and peace that comes from seeking God first. Ash Wednesday sets before us our false cisterns and the eternal fountain and says: 'Choose life.'

COLLECT
| Almighty and everlasting God,
you hate nothing that you have made
and forgive the sins of all those who are penitent:
create and make in us new and contrite hearts
that we, worthily lamenting our sins
and acknowledging our wretchedness,
may receive from you, the God of all mercy,
perfect remission and forgiveness;
through Jesus Christ your Son our Lord,
who is alive and reigns with you,
in the unity of the Holy Spirit,
one God, now and for ever.

Reflection by **Kate Bruce**

Psalm **77** *or* **78.1-39***
Jeremiah 2.14-32
John 4.1-26

Thursday 23 February

Jeremiah 2.14-32

'... long ago you broke your yoke and burst your bonds' (v.20)

Variously, Judah was a vassal of Assyria, Egypt and finally Babylon, in an era of political ferment. Jeremiah berates the people for pursuing Assyria and quaffing the waters of the Nile. They seek protection from that which is not God. Here is a spiritual tendency with which we can readily identify.

Jesus stated, that 'My yoke is easy and my burden is light' (Matthew 11.30). How readily we throw this yoke off and saddle ourselves with unhelpful baggage. We see this when we flee from God and rely on the weak crutches of our dependencies and competencies.

Apostacy is the flagrant refusal to follow the steer of Christ's yoke. We see it in the Church when political leaders are courted for power and patronage, even when their values and behaviour are obviously incompatible with the gospel. We see this in many examples of people victimized in order to protect the brand of big-name leaders and the cult of success.

Forsaking God's path is 'evil and bitter'. Don't trust Egypt or Assyria. No good thing can come of it. Rather, trust the one who said: 'Come to me, all you that are weary and are carrying heavy burdens, and I will give you rest. Take my yoke upon you, and learn from me; for I am gentle and humble in heart, and you will find rest for your souls.' (Matthew 11.28-29)

Holy God,
our lives are laid open before you:
rescue us from the chaos of sin
and through the death of your Son
bring us healing and make us whole
in Jesus Christ our Lord.

COLLECT

Reflection by **Kate Bruce**

Friday 24 February

Jeremiah 3.6-22

'I will heal your faithlessness.' (v.22)

There were two sisters: Israel, who lived in the north, and Judah who dwelt in the south. Israel did as she pleased and thus destroyed the one relationship that really mattered. Judah looked on, but learned nothing from her sister's situation. Judah pleased herself. When things looked bad, she put on a penitent act. Israel had no example to follow, but Judah did – and hence had less excuse for her disobedience and dissembling.

Judah presents an acceptable face. This ties in with the historic reforms of King Josiah, designed to bring Judah back to God. He was a man after God's heart, but his reforms did not bring about deep transformation in the spiritual life of the nation. Sunday best to look the part, but 'the Lord looks on the heart' (1 Samuel 16.7).

When you look at my heart, God, what do you see?

We are messy and muddled, and God knows this. There is no need to hide or dissemble before God. God sees us as we are and, like Israel and her sister, calls us to return, to be honest about our weakness and failure. God can work with this. It's the stubborn refusal to repent that blocks God, the insistence of false innocence that ties God's hands.

This Lent we cry out 'Create in me a clean heart, O God' (Psalm 51.10) and trust that God will heal our faithlessness.

C O L L E C T

Almighty and everlasting God,
you hate nothing that you have made
and forgive the sins of all those who are penitent:
create and make in us new and contrite hearts
that we, worthily lamenting our sins
and acknowledging our wretchedness,
may receive from you, the God of all mercy,
perfect remission and forgiveness;
through Jesus Christ your Son our Lord,
who is alive and reigns with you,
in the unity of the Holy Spirit,
one God, now and for ever.

| *Reflection by* **Kate Bruce**

Psalm **71** *or* **76**, 79
Jeremiah 4.1-18
John 4.43-end

Saturday 25 February

Jeremiah 4.1-18

'... or else my wrath will go forth like fire' (v.4)

Divine wrath? I'd rather dwell on the love of God, the warmth and welcome of God. But, airbrush out God's anger and we create a toothless deity. God is not a bit piqued because people aren't paying him attention. God is not a prima donna in a huff. God's fury comes because failure to worship causes evil to sprout up. Wickedness prospers and innocents pay.

We don't have to go far to see how neglect of God allows evil to flourish, but let's begin at home, with the Church. We have not protected children or the vulnerable. Throughout the worldwide Church, voices have been silenced in order not to sully reputations. Gender injustice is rife. Racism abounds. Difference is demonized. Do we care more about where the flower stand goes than about the plight of the hungry on the doorstep? As unpalatable as it is – this failure has its roots in not attending to the worship of God. I don't mean with bells and smells, or choruses and clapping; I mean in the deep places of the human heart.

Jeremiah offers this startling image: 'remove the foreskins of your heart.' Don't simply go through the motions of attending to right religious practice – circumcise your heart. In humility, bring the internal world of the self before God – that God might transform our vision, imagination, wounds, habits, attitude, language and action.

Holy God,
our lives are laid open before you:
rescue us from the chaos of sin
and through the death of your Son
bring us healing and make us whole
in Jesus Christ our Lord.

COLLECT

Reflection by **Kate Bruce**

11

Monday 27 February

Psalms 10, 11 *or* 80, 82
Jeremiah 4.19-end
John 5.1-18

Jeremiah 4.19-end

'They are skilled in doing evil, but do not know how to do good'
(v.22)

In the musical *Oliver*, Fagin sings about reviewing his situation. He's always been a robber – can he change? He examines what this might mean but is anxious about it. He concludes: 'I'm a bad 'un and a bad 'un I shall stay!' He elects to stick with the security of the life he knows. He is a pickpocket and villain; skilled in doing evil, he does not know how to do good.

To be skilled takes focus and practice. The people of God have intentionally decided not to know God. This causes Jeremiah deep anguish. He sees the coming judgement, the boiling pot from the north tipping over (1.13). Enemies will lay waste to cities, as desolation comes upon the land. Ultimately, the northern power, Babylon, a tool of divine judgement, carried the people into exile.

God wants his people to return to him, and his judgement – hard though it is – aims to bring them back from the stupidity of evil into restored relationship. Like Fagin they resist. The consequences will be terrible. But even in the depths of this horror, we find a diamond of hope. God is clear, judgement will come, but a doorway of light glimmers. 'I will not make a full end.' Given the deliberate evil of the people, who deserve only condemnation, God's grace is striking.

Is it time to review our situation?

COLLECT

Almighty God,
whose Son Jesus Christ fasted forty days in the wilderness,
and was tempted as we are, yet without sin:
give us grace to discipline ourselves in obedience to your Spirit;
and, as you know our weakness,
so may we know your power to save;
through Jesus Christ your Son our Lord,
who is alive and reigns with you,
in the unity of the Holy Spirit,
one God, now and for ever.

Reflection by **Kate Bruce**

Psalm **44** *or* 87, **89.1-18**
Jeremiah 5.1-19
John 5.19-29

Tuesday 28 February

Jeremiah 5.1-19

'They have spoken falsely of the Lord ...' (v.12)

Our reading today plunges us further into God's fury and anguish on the lips of Jeremiah. Rich and poor alike have abandoned God, setting their faces against repentance. Jeremiah is clear that this attitude will have a consequence, but the people delude themselves into believing that God winks at their apostasy.

Buckle up. Jeremiah's words demand our attention and pose hard questions. In honesty, we may find we have more in common with the people Jeremiah is addressing than we like to admit. Wherever we find ourselves today, God comes calling. 'Do not forsake me. Whatever you face, do not shut me out. Do not fool yourself that you can rely on your own resources. Do not speak falsely of me.'

Now is a good moment to remind ourselves that we draw breath because God gives us life. Our heart beats because God wills it so. Without God we are dust. Where our hearts are stony and rebellious, cry out to God to train and discipline them. When we see the clay of our life as a misshapen pot, cry that the potter would throw us on the wheel and remake us.

God can do nothing with a rebellious heart, but a penitent spirit is malleable. God of grace – remake us.

Heavenly Father,
your Son battled with the powers of darkness,
and grew closer to you in the desert:
help us to use these days to grow in wisdom and prayer
that we may witness to your saving love
in Jesus Christ our Lord.

COLLECT

Reflection by **Kate Bruce** | 13

Wednesday 1 March

Psalms **6**, 17 *or* **119.105-128**
Jeremiah 5.20-end
John 5.30-end

Jeremiah 5.20-end

'... your sins have deprived you of good' (v.25)

When the Tempter crooks a beckoning finger, it always whispers attraction. 'This will be good. This will be pleasing. This will satisfy.' Imagine you are desperately thirsty; the Tempter offers to quench your need with a mug of liquid. Anticipating relief, you gulp it down. It is always brine. Our sins always deprive us of good, even if they come with the promise of great reward. Ponder the temptation of Jesus in the wilderness, which can be summed up as: 'feed yourself and please yourself'. Clear-sighted, Jesus tipped the brine away.

The devil dances to a discordant beat. When we attend to this cacophony, we become deaf to heaven's music: the songs of faith, hope and love, the tunes of kindness, compassion and generosity fade away. Jeremiah's audience are gyrating to a destructive rhythm: thieving and treachery are the norm; the rich have grown fat and sleek in their corruption; the religious leaders are weak and false; the land is in peril. Revelling in their sense of superior selfhood, none realize the proximity of the axe of judgement.

Open a news app and skim the headlines. It is not difficult to see how sin, individual and societal, creates cultures in which the vulnerable are preyed upon, where the powerful line their own pockets, and where truth is spun to say what suits.

Jeremiah speaks truth: sin will always deprive us of ultimate good.

COLLECT

Almighty God,
whose Son Jesus Christ fasted forty days in the wilderness,
and was tempted as we are, yet without sin:
give us grace to discipline ourselves in obedience to your Spirit;
and, as you know our weakness,
so may we know your power to save;
through Jesus Christ your Son our Lord,
who is alive and reigns with you,
in the unity of the Holy Spirit,
one God, now and for ever.

Reflection by **Kate Bruce**

Psalms **42**, 43 *or* 90, **92**
Jeremiah 6.9-21
John 6.1-15

Thursday 2 March

Jeremiah 6.9-21

'They have treated the wound of my people carelessly' (v.14)

Remember the asphalt surfaces of school playgrounds? If you fell, tiny bits of stone embedded themselves in scraped knees. Being patched up involved the painful removal of this grit from the graze, with the ubiquitous, stingy application of witch hazel. Wounds cleaned up by kind hands.

We are far enough into Jeremiah's book to know that the wound he mentions is more grievous than a scraped knee; there is raging infection in the land, a pandemic transmitted by dishonesty, disorder and denial. Economic dishonesty elevates the idol of greed. Apostasy ushers in spiritual disorder. The careless attitude of those tasked with tending the spiritual health of the people has fostered denial of the truth.

This wound needs a powerful salve: 'Look for the ancient paths, where the good way lies; and walk in it.' Jeremiah's primary audience ignored his words. Are *we* listening? This Lent, come back to the pathways of prayer, dive into the river of Scripture, submit to confession and spiritual direction.

We need the presence of God in the attentiveness of each other. It takes great courage to allow someone to tend our hidden wounds, but this is vital. Where we are honoured with such trust – there is no room for carelessness as we pick out the stubborn grit of sin and failure, bringing the sting of truth and the salve of kindness.

Heavenly Father,
your Son battled with the powers of darkness,
and grew closer to you in the desert:
help us to use these days to grow in wisdom and prayer
that we may witness to your saving love
in Jesus Christ our Lord.

COLLECT

Reflection by **Kate Bruce**   15

Friday 3 March

Jeremiah 6.22-end

'... mourning as for an only child, most bitter lamentation' (v.26)

In the Jewish Museum in Berlin is an art installation, *'Shalekhet'* ('Fallen Leaves'), by Menashe Kadishman. It consists of faces made from chunks of metal, piled on each other. You are invited to walk across them – a profoundly unsettling experience. They knock together making a sound like iron wheels on railway tracks. It's the sound of violence, oppression, theft, abuse, and terrible, terrible fear. It is the sound of exile.

In 586 BC, Judah experienced the culmination of a series of deportations. Nebuchadnezzar II of Babylon sacked Jerusalem and destroyed the temple. Judah is smashed politically, socially, economically and spiritually. Jeremiah sees this on the horizon, and states the uncomfortable truth: God has rejected them. It is the cry of exile.

The only response to this devastation is honest, bitter lament. This is not how things should be. What have we done? Where is God? Lament prevents us from running too quickly to Pollyanna-ish declarations of hope: the 'peace, peace, when there is no peace' (Jeremiah 6.14) of the false prophets. This simply hides the wounds and silences those who know first hand the absence of peace.

However, lament does not keep us trapped forever in the despair of exile, or trouble of any kind. Lament is a doorway into hope, because it is spoken to someone. It is addressed to God: 'How long, *O Lord.*' That's the point of exile.

COLLECT

Almighty God,
whose Son Jesus Christ fasted forty days in the wilderness,
and was tempted as we are, yet without sin:
give us grace to discipline ourselves in obedience to your Spirit;
and, as you know our weakness,
so may we know your power to save;
through Jesus Christ your Son our Lord,
who is alive and reigns with you,
in the unity of the Holy Spirit,
one God, now and for ever.

Reflection by **Kate Bruce**

Psalms 59, **63** *or* 96, **97**, 100
Jeremiah 7.1-20
John 6.27-40

Saturday 4 March

Jeremiah 7.1-20

'Do not trust in these deceptive words: "This is the temple of the Lord, the temple of the Lord, the temple of the Lord."' (v.4)

Imagine someone standing outside a place of worship, declaring that Sunday best and rote liturgical chuntering are deceptive, as is the requisite repetition of choruses or the intonation of psalms, *if the heart is absent from worship*. Their voice cuts through the inevitably frosty response with a reminder that God desires reformation of the heart, no more attending worship one day and offering cakes to idols the next. You're imagining Jeremiah.

'Let me dwell with you in this place' says God. Has God been pushed out of his own temple? The idea of God dwelling with his people is present in Revelation 21, in an intimate picture: 'See the home of God is among mortals. He will dwell with them; they will be his peoples' (Revelation 21.3). Like Jeremiah's audience, we are being called into this intimate, uncompromising relationship with God. You can't hobble between God and your preferred idol. The idols have to go.

Perhaps we find it difficult to let go of our props and supports? Then tell God about this.

We cannot transform ourselves, but we can be open to the transformative power of God dwelling in us. God speaks persistently – we must respond, even if that response is simply: 'God help me. Remake me. Potter, throw me on your wheel again.'

Heavenly Father,
your Son battled with the powers of darkness,
and grew closer to you in the desert:
help us to use these days to grow in wisdom and prayer
that we may witness to your saving love
in Jesus Christ our Lord.

COLLECT

Monday 6 March

Jeremiah 7.21-end

'Obey my voice, and I will be your God' (v.23)

Many years ago, there was a production of the musical *Godspell* that began with a number of actors coming to the front of the stage and singing loudly about their philosophy of life. One sang about capitalism, one about socialism, another about humanism, and so on. Their songs started to conflict with eath other and made such a racket that the audience didn't know who to listen to any more. All of a sudden, a very loud ram's horn sounded, and in walked a man carrying a bucket of water. He began splashing it around, first on the actors and then on everyone else. It was John the Baptist, and he was telling us to wash our mouths and ears out, and to prepare ourselves to hear the one true song that really matters.

John was in the tradition of prophets like Jeremiah. In today's reading, we find Jeremiah voicing God's desire for his people to hear him, to listen to his melodies of fidelity and peace, so that they can wake up to who they have become, and to the destructive and inhumane things they are doing. Alarmingly, we discover this includes the ritual sacrifice of children.

In all the noise of now, it can be hard to hear yourself, or the world that is making you. Jeremiah reminds us that at such a time, truth can perish and there will be a lot of collateral damage in our relationships and society.

COLLECT

Almighty God,
you show to those who are in error the light of your truth,
that they may return to the way of righteousness:
grant to all those who are admitted
    into the fellowship of Christ's religion,
that they may reject those things
    that are contrary to their profession,
and follow all such things as are agreeable to the same;
through our Lord Jesus Christ,
who is alive and reigns with you,
in the unity of the Holy Spirit,
one God, now and for ever.

Reflection by **Mark Oakley**

Psalm **50** *or* **106*** (*or* 103)
Jeremiah 8.1-15
John 6.52-59

Tuesday 7 March

Jeremiah 8.1-15

'... they did not know how to blush' (v.12)

In the poetry of this chapter, Jeremiah relates God's bewilderment at his people as he identifies what is at the heart of their problems. They have 'held fast to deceit', 'do not speak honestly', and, like horses charging into battle, are blind to the dangers facing them. At the same time as all this, people like to think of themselves as wise and peaceful and so have no ability to self-scrutinize. They don't even blush at their behaviour.

Towards the end of today's passage, it seems to dawn on folk that the crisis in which they find themselves may be caught up in the way they have been living their lives. It feels as if God may be punishing them and therefore they are, at last, prompted to ask 'what for?'

It is easy in life to conclude from time to time that God 'has given us poisoned water to drink' as some divine retribution on us. What is harder to see is that so often we bring pain on ourselves, that our behaviour can catch up with us, that hidden truths come to light, that relationships break down as people begin to see who we really are or what we've been up to.

Sometimes, life throws things at us out of the blue, but at other times, we are simply victims of our own worst selves.

Almighty God,
by the prayer and discipline of Lent
may we enter into the mystery of Christ's sufferings,
and by following in his Way
come to share in his glory;
through Jesus Christ our Lord.

COLLECT

Reflection by **Mark Oakley**   19

Wednesday 8 March

Jeremiah 8.18 – 9.11

'O that my head were a spring of water, and my eyes a fountain of tears' (9.1)

There is scholarly debate as to who is speaking and crying in this passage. Is it Jeremiah asking us to hear 'the cry of my own poor people'? Or is it a personified Jerusalem whose 'joy is gone'? Or maybe it is the people themselves acknowledging that 'for the hurt of my poor people I am hurt'? However, for some, it is as clear as day that it is God who is weeping, pained by the fact that those he loves 'refuse to know me'. As evidence of this, Jeremiah cites the deceit, selfishness and hypocrisy of atomized individuals who have no commitment to God's vision for human society and the principles that are required to bring it into reality.

Tears are mentioned a few times here. Today, they can be something we try to hide. We worry that they expose our vulnerability, need, or deep unhappiness, in a world in which we are supposed to have none of these things. In the Christian tradition, however, tears are often greeted as a gift. They are eloquent and honest. They bypass the words we can use to hide and reveal our soul, to others and to ourselves, unfiltered.

The poet and priest John Donne prayed in one of his Holy Sonnets, in the spirit of Jeremiah, that, as 'a little world made cunningly', tears might drown his destructive worldview and wash his eyes out to see, and to live, better.

COLLECT

Almighty God,
you show to those who are in error the light of your truth,
that they may return to the way of righteousness:
grant to all those who are admitted
    into the fellowship of Christ's religion,
that they may reject those things
    that are contrary to their profession,
and follow all such things as are agreeable to the same;
through our Lord Jesus Christ,
who is alive and reigns with you,
in the unity of the Holy Spirit,
one God, now and for ever.

Reflection by **Mark Oakley**

Thursday 9 March

Jeremiah 9.12-24

*'I act with steadfast love, justice, and righteousness in the earth,
for in these things I delight' (v.24)*

When the writer and theologian Ronald Knox was told by a friend to 'pull himself together', Knox replied: 'I'm not sure I have a together.' This experience in which we feel we lack an integrated or centred self, as individuals or as a community, is at the heart of what is known as 'lament'. When something happens to us that shatters our view of things, and which doesn't fit in with our outlook on life, we need to move slowly towards appropriating what has happened so that our view of things changes, widens, to include our new experience. This move is often painful and costly. To help it along, we lament.

To lament means to be honest about the hurt of our world crashing around us, about the anger we may feel, or the doubt in a God who would do such a thing. The purpose of lament, in the spiritual life, is to help get us back to a place of praise.

In today's reading, God calls on 'the mourning-women to come'. He invites their 'dirge' so that 'eyes may run down with tears'. It is only through such lament that his people will recognize what exile and loss has done to them and, then, how it might be shaped into a new life where they will understand and know him.

Almighty God,
by the prayer and discipline of Lent
may we enter into the mystery of Christ's sufferings,
and by following in his Way
come to share in his glory;
through Jesus Christ our Lord.

COLLECT

Reflection by **Mark Oakley** | 21

Friday 10 March

Psalms 40, **41** *or* **139**
Jeremiah 10.1-16
John 7.14-24

Jeremiah 10.1-16

'There is none like you, O Lord' (v.6)

Today's reading makes a similar point to that found in Psalm 115. The gods worshipped in Jeremiah's day are 'like scarecrows'; they are human creations in a human likeness, and we set them up to be adored. In doing so, it is ourselves that we end up bowing down to. In contrast, we are told here that there is none like the Lord and that 'he is the living God'. The gods of others might be made of silver and gold, but there are many things more valuable than money. Of supreme value is to know the true God, who made the earth with wisdom, and to understand that other substitutes we pursue will always let us down because 'they are worthless, a work of delusion'.

One might read the book of Jeremiah and conclude that God is to be feared because he is fierce and out to punish us. What Jeremiah is teaching, though, is that we are not to worship God because he is vindictive, but because he is real. We find this reality hard to bear because so much of our own composition is made up of cover-ups, superficialities and avoidances. So we replace the reality of God with a range of convenient replacements – and for some of us this might be the self-congratulation of being part of the 'right' religion – but all of them must fall away if we are to stand before the 'the true God' to see, and be seen, with the transparent and faithful eyes of love.

COLLECT

Almighty God,
you show to those who are in error the light of your truth,
that they may return to the way of righteousness:
grant to all those who are admitted
    into the fellowship of Christ's religion,
that they may reject those things
    that are contrary to their profession,
and follow all such things as are agreeable to the same;
through our Lord Jesus Christ,
who is alive and reigns with you,
in the unity of the Holy Spirit,
one God, now and for ever.

Reflection by **Mark Oakley**

Psalms 3, **25** *or* 120, **121**, 122
Jeremiah 10.17-24
John 7.25-36

Saturday 11 March

Jeremiah 10.17-24

'Correct me, O Lord, but in just measure' (v.24)

The hurt voice of an exiled people is loud in this passage. They see they have forgotten life-giving truths, that their leaders have wounded them, and that now they are all scattered. They can sense what lies ahead. The severity of their wound, and exile, must now be borne, it seems, as a punishment for their confident stupidity in ignoring the covenant with their God. Perhaps if they repent, they reflect, God will eventually also punish those who have laid waste their land and homes?

The prayer at the end of this passage is that they might be corrected, but in just measure and not in anger. It is a courageous thing to pray to be amended because, as the great truths of our faith remind us, there has to be a fall before there is a redemption, and death before life. In other words, if we are to be rescued there needs to be some rupture; salvation is a 'falling awake', as it were.

If our prayer is that we be changed, are we prepared? What needs to be lost if we ourselves are not to be lost in a maze of our own making?

Almighty God,
by the prayer and discipline of Lent
may we enter into the mystery of Christ's sufferings,
and by following in his Way
come to share in his glory;
through Jesus Christ our Lord.

COLLECT

Reflection by **Mark Oakley** | 23

Monday 13 March

Psalms **5**, 7 *or* 123, 124, 125, **126**
Jeremiah 11.1-17
John 7.37-52

Jeremiah 11.1-17

'What right has my beloved in my house, when she has done vile deeds? (v.15)

Today's passage is sometimes known as Jeremiah's 'covenant sermon'. His message is that people should listen again to God because they have an extraordinary ability to ignore the lessons of the past and so repeat the mistakes of their ancestors in following other gods. It is a radical sermon because Jeremiah announces the collapse of the Mosaic covenant on account of this disloyalty. This covenant is rooted in the promise that, if the people are faithful to him, God will always be their God and will give them a land to build their community life in. However, just as they decide not to listen to God anymore, so God now refuses to listen to them. Their relationship is shattered.

Anyone who has gone through a painful separation with a lover knows what chaotic emotions take over. They range from regret or shame, to hate, hurt and fantasies of revenge. Nothing is more dislocating that the departure of someone you had built hopes and dreams with. What happens to your unemployed love, now? We speak, at such times, of our hearts 'breaking'.

So, it seems, does God, who makes a comparison with such a break-up and to the perplexed heartache it creates.

COLLECT

Almighty God,
whose most dear Son went not up to joy
    but first he suffered pain,
and entered not into glory before he was crucified:
mercifully grant that we, walking in the way of the cross,
may find it none other than the way of life and peace;
through Jesus Christ your Son our Lord,
who is alive and reigns with you,
in the unity of the Holy Spirit,
one God, now and for ever.

| *Reflection by* **Mark Oakley**

Psalms 6, **9** *or* **132**, 133
Jeremiah 11.18 – 12.6
John 7.53 – 8.11

Tuesday 14 March

Jeremiah 11.18 – 12.6

'... you are near in their mouths yet far from their hearts' (12.2)

The clear theme that emerges here is that of divine justice. Jeremiah lays out something of his inner life, and how it feels, as a prophet, like being a lamb led to slaughter. By sharing his feelings, we see that Jeremiah both embodies the pain of his exiled people, and the pain of his God, who is being ignored by those he loves and made a covenant with. Jeremiah symbolizes both his community and his God, representing each to the other, and so bears the cost of the one asked to help repair their relationship.

Jeremiah is asking why he finds himself the victim of devised schemes, but he is also asking questions as to why the unpleasant and guilty people seem to flourish in life. Jeremiah is frustrated at how so many are treacherous, but he concedes that God still made them, even though God is now 'far from their hearts'.

Today we can find ourselves asking similar questions about why it is that the good can suffer and the wicked do quite nicely. What matters ultimately is the quality of the human heart, and our ability to love rather than judge our neighbour. By loving, we counter all that works against what is just and begin to become the answer to our own questions about God's way of shaping this world.

Eternal God,
give us insight
to discern your will for us,
to give up what harms us,
and to seek the perfection we are promised
in Jesus Christ our Lord.

COLLECT

Reflection by **Mark Oakley**

Wednesday 15 March

Psalm **38** *or* **119.153-end**
Jeremiah 13.1-11
John 8.12-30

Jeremiah 13.1-11

'... now the loincloth was ruined; it was good for nothing' (v.7)

This is a bit strange. It sounds as if God is asking Jeremiah to go and hide a pair of his pants in the earth, by the water, and wait for them to be unwearable. That appears to be exactly what Jeremiah does. Perhaps we need some weird behaviour by people of faith to break through the 'common sense' articulacy of a culture that is misguided and headed for ruin? I look forward to the preachers of today using a pair of Y-fronts to challenge the misguided decisions of government!

The prophetic act here is serious, though. God is asking his people to see that he 'clings' to them, like thin material on sweat, but in 'stubbornly following their own will', they are losing their identity as a community and becoming purposeless. This pride of theirs needs dealing with if they are to see sense and become 'a people, a name, a praise, and a glory' that he has always longed for them to be. If it takes burying a loincloth to understand the depths of God's frustration, and the ways he will prise them away from their ridiculous gods, then so be it.

How we do the same in our own day is a challenge to how imaginative our discipleship is, or should be.

COLLECT

Almighty God,
whose most dear Son went not up to joy
   but first he suffered pain,
and entered not into glory before he was crucified:
mercifully grant that we, walking in the way of the cross,
may find it none other than the way of life and peace;
through Jesus Christ your Son our Lord,
who is alive and reigns with you,
in the unity of the Holy Spirit,
one God, now and for ever.

Reflection by **Mark Oakley**

Psalms **56**, 57 *or* **143**, 146
Jeremiah 14
John 8.31-47

Thursday 16 March

Jeremiah 14

'... we are called by your name' (v.9)

The second half of verse 9 is often read at the late night office of Compline. In the stillness, surrounded by encroaching darkness and with a long night ahead, the congregation prays to the Lord who is 'in the midst of us' and asks that he does not forsake them. Similarly, we find in the poetry of today's passage, a people who have become aware of their own sins and who can't breathe in the frightening atmosphere of their own creation. They need God, and now they see that need. They ask that God will not be like some 'stranger' to them.

The reading today begins with the image of drought and thirst. Everyone – including the animals and environment – is thirsty and needs water if hope is to be restored. This is a spiritual metaphor, of course, and yet God alerts Jeremiah to the fact that at a time when people are longing for refreshment, false prophets come along and say everything is all right. At the risk of sounding like some vengeful and capricious deity, God nevertheless has to reveal the severity of the situation before any change is possible. Out of the calamity comes the heartfelt cry from his people, 'remember and do not break your covenant with us'.

Eternal God,
give us insight
to discern your will for us,
to give up what harms us,
and to seek the perfection we are promised
in Jesus Christ our Lord.

COLLECT

Reflection by **Mark Oakley** | 27

Friday 17 March

Jeremiah 15.10-end

'... utter what is precious, and not what is worthless' (v.19)

In the Church of England's *Book of Common Prayer*, there is a collect that asks that we might 'inwardly digest' Scripture, God's nutritious word. In Jeremiah's lament, which we read today, he says that he has eaten the language of God, made inseparable from him, so that he can make God's vision known to his contemporaries. The problem is, he continues, this has made him a lonely figure and given him a life of unceasing pain. He audaciously takes God on about this, complaining that God appears to be a deceitful brook that has dried up and stopped giving.

God's reply is to the point. Look at me, keep your eyes on me, speak what is precious – and then people will turn to you for help in their renewed search for me. Some will still not like you, Jeremiah, but you will overcome this with me by your side.

Just as we are told before a plane takes off that, should there be difficulty, we should place the oxygen mask over ourselves before assisting others, we need to breathe if we are to help others survive, so Jeremiah learns that he needs to be spiritually resourced and fortified by God, before he will have any authenticity or plausibility among a distracted and hungry people.

COLLECT

Almighty God,
whose most dear Son went not up to joy
    but first he suffered pain,
and entered not into glory before he was crucified:
mercifully grant that we, walking in the way of the cross,
may find it none other than the way of life and peace;
through Jesus Christ your Son our Lord,
who is alive and reigns with you,
in the unity of the Holy Spirit,
one God, now and for ever.

Reflection by **Mark Oakley**

Saturday 18 March

Jeremiah 16.10 – 17.4

'O Lord, my strength and my stronghold' (16.19)

The questions raised in this passage are those that lie at the heart of the book of Jeremiah: What have we done wrong? Why are we suffering? What do we need to do? God's reply to Jeremiah is clear. The people have forsaken him and followed other gods, not keeping his law, and their selfish pursuits have reached the inevitable consequence of leaving them confused and without any compass. There is nothing new in this; they are acting like their ancestors, but they are the more foolish for not having learned a better way than them.

In the middle of all this distress, we find in verses 19 and 20 a voice breaking into the chaos that is loyal and confident. It is a voice of calm and trusting faithfulness, speaking intimately with God as 'strength', 'stronghold' and 'refuge'. The voice acknowledges the lies of the past and the worthless pursuits that have led the generations into barren and desperate places, even, on the way, making gods in the image of themselves.

As we read Jeremiah's pages, with its laments, questions, hurt and loss – both God's and his deported people's – such a voice shows us a pool of light, a relationship that imbues a true sense of identity again, built on renewing trust and instilling peace.

Eternal God,
give us insight
to discern your will for us,
to give up what harms us,
and to seek the perfection we are promised
in Jesus Christ our Lord.

COLLECT

Reflection by **Mark Oakley**

Monday 20 March
Joseph of Nazareth

Psalms 25, 147.1-12
Isaiah 11.1-10
Matthew 13.54-end

Matthew 13.54–end

'… is this not the carpenter's son?' (v.55)

Matthew describes Jesus as 'the carpenter's son'. This visit by Jesus to his home town, Nazareth, is recorded in almost identical words in Mark's Gospel, except there Jesus is called 'the carpenter'.

In his commentary on the New Testament, eminent theologian Anthony Harvey wondered whether this change was significant. Was Matthew revealing a reluctance on the part of the first Christians to acknowledge that Jesus had been a tradesman? It seems unlikely there was much of that sort of class snobbery around in first century Galilee. In any case, being a carpenter was quite respectable. A good carpenter is rarely out of work.

This tangential reference to Joseph (perhaps still alive when Jesus began his ministry) is all the more valuable because otherwise he disappears from the Gospels after the family visit to Jerusalem when Jesus was twelve. We're reminded here that Jesus was part of an ordinary human family for three decades. The names of his brothers – James, Joseph, Simon and Judas – are mentioned. Sometimes we speak of 'the holy family' as if it consisted only of Mary, Joseph and Jesus. It's the very ordinariness of his wider family that makes people think Jesus cannot be the Messiah. This is another reminder that those who witnessed the incarnation were blindest to it, just as we are so frequently unable to see God in the lives of those closest to us. Where may we see him in our life today?

COLLECT

God our Father,
who from the family of your servant David
raised up Joseph the carpenter
to be the guardian of your incarnate Son
and husband of the Blessed Virgin Mary:
give us grace to follow him
in faithful obedience to your commands;
through Jesus Christ your Son our Lord,
who is alive and reigns with you,
in the unity of the Holy Spirit,
one God, now and for ever.

30 | *Reflection by* **Graham James**

Psalms 54, **79** *or* **5**, 6 (8)
Jeremiah 18.1-12
John 10.1-10

Tuesday 21 March

Jeremiah 18.1-12

'... he reworked it into another vessel' (v.4)

I visited a pottery where I was invited to have a go at the potter's wheel. I showed no natural talent. It took a long time, and a good many reworkings, to produce anything that looked vaguely like a bowl. But the benefit of clay was that I could take what was misshapen, roll it up and start again.

I remember being told to work *with* the clay, and to avoid too much pressure (or too little). Clay may be malleable, but you cannot do just what you please with it. Clay can be resistant to the potter's hands. It definitely was to mine. While the potter determines how the clay is shaped, the character of clay means it's a process in which the good potter respects the clay and its inherent qualities.

In using this image of the potter and the clay, Jeremiah is illustrating the undoubted sovereignty of God. But this is not a God unresponsive to his people, imposing himself without regard for them. This is a God who says he may change his mind and who will remake his people if they amend their ways.

When I watch a potter at work, it is the deep respect for the material that I notice, a tenderness and respect for the recalcitrant clay. That's why this image remains such a powerful and moving reminder of a God who is always prepared to rework us into a better shape.

COLLECT

Merciful Lord,
absolve your people from their offences,
that through your bountiful goodness
we may all be delivered from the chains of those sins
which by our frailty we have committed;
grant this, heavenly Father,
for Jesus Christ's sake, our blessed Lord and Saviour,
who is alive and reigns with you,
in the unity of the Holy Spirit,
one God, now and for ever.

Reflection by **Graham James**

31

Wednesday 22 March

Jeremiah 18.13-end

'... let us make plots against Jeremiah' (v.18)

Although in our contemporary world, biblical knowledge is not what it was, someone forecasting disaster may still be described as a 'Jeremiah'. Today's reading tells us why. Jeremiah's prophecies of doom for Israel continued for around 30 years, and so his credibility waned. If Jeremiah was really speaking words from the Lord, why did nothing happen? The priests and leading figures among the people of Israel got fed up having their integrity impugned so they plotted to destroy Jeremiah's reputation. Why should he not get a taste of his own medicine?

Jeremiah, aware of the plotting against him, pleads with the Lord to act. God may have his reasons for being patient with his faithless people, but within Jeremiah himself there's a longing that the Lord should not 'forgive their iniquity'.

There are two features of the human condition vividly reflected here. The first is the way in which we long to strike back at those who are our severest critics. Sometimes we know in our hearts that what they say has a measure of truth. That may make us even more angry and resentful. Was that the case with Jeremiah's opponents?

When we are in the right, however, and face opposition, we may want to see our critics face retribution. That's dangerous too since we become judgemental, usurping God's place. Righteousness can morph into self-righteousness. Being resentful or becoming self-righteous. Neither is attractive. Which is the greater danger in our own lives?

COLLECT

Merciful Lord,
absolve your people from their offences,
that through your bountiful goodness
we may all be delivered from the chains of those sins
which by our frailty we have committed;
grant this, heavenly Father,
for Jesus Christ's sake, our blessed Lord and Saviour,
who is alive and reigns with you,
in the unity of the Holy Spirit,
one God, now and for ever.

Reflection by **Graham James**

Psalms 53, **86** *or* 14, **15**, 16
Jeremiah 19.1-13
John 10.22-end

Thursday 23 March

Jeremiah 19.1-13

'... you shall break the jug' (v.10)

Broken pottery litters archaeological sites in the Middle East. Pots were frequently broken and thrown away. But Jeremiah takes a perfectly good jug, and in the presence of the senior priests and elders of the people, smashes it as an acted metaphor that the Lord is going to destroy the faithless people and their city too. Unlike the image used in the previous chapter in which the clay could be reworked, this vessel 'can never be mended'. It's a bleak prospect.

Over a decade ago at a service in Norwich Cathedral, the preacher gave his text, and as people settled in their seats, he took a glazed pot and threw it from the pulpit onto the stone floor in front of the nave altar. The robed clergy in the vicinity looked as shattered as the pot. The preacher was not re-enacting Jeremiah's action but drawing attention to St Paul describing himself and his fellow Christians as no better than 'earthen vessels' (2 Corinthians 4.7, KJV) to contain the treasure of the gospel. Fragile, cracked and misshapen we may be, the preacher said, but God takes, mends and remakes us.

History shows us that societies and civilizations do break apart, never to be mended. But peoples, including the people of Israel, are made and remade. God has a habit of being tender to the broken. What brokenness in us needs to be remade today?

COLLECT

Merciful Lord,
you know our struggle to serve you:
when sin spoils our lives
and overshadows our hearts,
come to our aid
and turn us back to you again;
through Jesus Christ our Lord.

Reflection by **Graham James**

Friday 24 March

Jeremiah 19.14 – 20.6

'The Lord has named you … "Terror-all-around".' (20.3)

It was after the destruction of the twin towers of the World Trade Center in New York in 2001 and the tragic loss of so many lives that the United States President spoke of a 'war on terror'. Even at the time, some commentators wondered how war could be waged on an abstraction. It soon became clear that it would be a war against terrorists and the nations that harboured, trained or encouraged them. Osama bin Laden himself embodied this terror.

Jeremiah tells us that Pashur was the chief officer in the temple. He would have been in charge of security and expected to keep the peace in the house of the Lord. Jeremiah saw how the temple had become home to foreign cults and wayward teaching. He renames Pashur and calls him 'Terror-all-around'. It's another symbolic action, like the smashing of the jar. Pashur will be enveloped in the terror that's to come upon the people of Judah. He will be at the epicentre of that terror and is now the very embodiment of it.

We don't hear Pashur's side of this story. Pashur may have been simply trying to do his job. He may not have been able to see beyond his situation. Jeremiah is hoping to open his eyes, but even more to warn the people of Judah about the fate that awaited them. How easy it is for us to have our eyes open but fail to see what God demands of us.

COLLECT

Merciful Lord,
absolve your people from their offences,
that through your bountiful goodness
we may all be delivered from the chains of those sins
which by our frailty we have committed;
grant this, heavenly Father,
for Jesus Christ's sake, our blessed Lord and Saviour,
who is alive and reigns with you,
in the unity of the Holy Spirit,
one God, now and for ever.

Reflection by **Graham James**

Psalms 111, 113
I Samuel 2.1-10
Romans 5.12-end

Saturday 25 March
Annunciation of Our Lord
to the Blessed Virgin Mary

Romans 5.12-end

'... grace abounded all the more' (v.20)

It is surprising how often the word 'grace' is used in the English-speaking world today. An actor may be praised for performing with grace; a secretary replying on behalf of the Queen may say she has been 'graciously pleased' to receive a gift; and an invocation before a meal is called grace. Church meetings end frequently with everyone saying the Grace – words adapted from 2 Corinthians 13.13, where Paul refers to 'the grace of the Lord Jesus Christ...' In one dictionary I consulted, there were 16 different definitions of this single word 'grace'.

Apart from when someone is accused of having 'airs and graces', the definitions are positive. Elegance, beauty, goodwill: these are connected with grace. The gracious person is favoured. It's no surprise that the angel hails Mary at the Annunciation by telling her that she is favoured, 'full of grace', as many people throughout the Christian world say every day in their devotions. The Holy Spirit is to come upon Mary and enable her to have the grace (and strength) to give birth to Jesus.

Archbishop William Temple once reflected on the difficulty we experience if we are selfish and want to be unselfish. He said we need more than moral resolution to change. Something has to take hold of us from outside – the gift of grace. Grace 'abounds', as Paul testifies, and may bring God's favour into our lives today.

COLLECT

We beseech you, O Lord,
pour your grace into our hearts,
that as we have known the incarnation of your Son Jesus Christ
by the message of an angel,
so by his cross and passion
we may be brought to the glory of his resurrection;
through Jesus Christ your Son our Lord,
who is alive and reigns with you,
in the unity of the Holy Spirit,
one God, now and for ever.

Reflection by **Graham James**   35

Monday 27 March

Psalms **73**, 121 *or* 27, **30**
Jeremiah 21.1-10
John 11.28-44

Jeremiah 21.1-10

'... perform a wonderful deed for us' (v.2)

Since Jeremiah had prophesied doom for so long, it's surprising King Zedekiah would want to consult him when faced by Babylonian invaders. The Judean political and religious elite must have been desperate, but they cherished a hope that their God would 'perform a wonderful deed for us, as he has often done'. They remembered what God had done for their ancestors. Surely God would want to protect his name and his people?

Jeremiah also believed in the Lord's ability to do wonderful deeds. The temptation for him to say something pleasing may have been huge. But he had long believed the nation had rebelled so fully against God that its destruction was inevitable. Only this would lead to a radical rebuilding and a renewed trust in God. Jeremiah makes no political or military calculation before he speaks. He holds no brief for the Babylonians. He sees them simply as the instrument God has chosen by which the destruction will happen. Jeremiah speaks without consideration for his own wellbeing.

Some 2600 years separate us from Jeremiah. But ours remains a world in which individual courageous voices are heard in countries where prophetic words are not simply unwelcome but vigorously suppressed. In our everyday lives we know how challenging it is to say something unpopular and unwelcome, especially if we are in a tiny minority. Today, let us give thanks and pray for the prophets of our own age.

COLLECT

Most merciful God,
who by the death and resurrection of your Son Jesus Christ
delivered and saved the world:
grant that by faith in him who suffered on the cross
we may triumph in the power of his victory;
through Jesus Christ your Son our Lord,
who is alive and reigns with you,
in the unity of the Holy Spirit,
one God, now and for ever.

| *Reflection by* **Graham James**

Psalms **35**, 123 *or* 32, **36**
Jeremiah 22.1-5, 13-19
John 11.45-end

Tuesday 28 March

Jeremiah 22.1-5, 13-19
'Act with justice and righteousness ...' (v.3)

The book of Jeremiah is not chronological. In the last chapter we were in King Zedekiah's reign, and now we have gone back in time to his predecessor King Jehoiakim. But there's no distinction between them as far as the force of Jeremiah's condemnation is concerned.

Jeremiah expected a lot of the king of Judah because the nation's faithfulness to God's law and commandments rested upon the shoulders of the Davidic king. The king was to be exemplary in acting with righteousness and justice, protecting the widows and orphans, and those most vulnerable in the land. Jehoiakim had neglected these things and imagined the grandeur of his lavish lifestyle reflected divine approval. His father Josiah had lived well too (as did David himself), but Jeremiah says Josiah gave priority to judging 'the cause of the poor and the needy'. The Davidic monarchy was to be different from that of other nations because it was a living expression of God's covenant with his people.

The expectation of exemplary character in monarchs has lasted to the present day. Many have been far from worthy but the expectation is still there. Even a constitutional monarch with very little political power may be looked upon as the protector of all that is just and right. The monarch is called to be the servant of the people as well as the embodiment of the nation. That's a sacred trust.

COLLECT

Gracious Father,
you gave up your Son
out of love for the world:
lead us to ponder the mysteries of his passion,
that we may know eternal peace
through the shedding of our Saviour's blood,
Jesus Christ our Lord.

Reflection by **Graham James** | 37

Wednesday 29 March

Jeremiah 22.20 – 23.8

'I ... will gather the remnant of my flock' (23.3)

After so much unremitting condemnation, it comes as a relief that Jeremiah changes his tone. Although he puts no trust in Judah's kings and their heirs, he does point to a day when God will raise up a 'righteous Branch' from the line of David to restore justice and righteousness in a renewed nation.

But there are years of pain to come first. Jeremiah anticipates both the exile of the people in Babylon and their return. He suggests that this return will be so wonderful that it will even displace the exodus from Egypt in the memory of God's people. These exiles will be the ones to build the nation again, not those who remain in Jerusalem living under whatever conditions the Babylonians impose.

The experience of being dispossessed and subjugated in exile will be a school of learning and renewal. Those who suffer the most will learn the most. And from them true shepherds of God's people will be found. When we are burdened and sad, to whom do we go for support? Is it to the brash and self-confident who seem to sail through life? It's unlikely. We go to the person who has suffered themselves, who is attentive and not over-powering, who listens and loves.

Churches rarely ask for the broken and suffering to shepherd them. Yet it is usually the broken and the suffering they get, whoever they've asked for. They make the best shepherds of Christ's flock.

COLLECT

Most merciful God,
who by the death and resurrection of your Son Jesus Christ
delivered and saved the world:
grant that by faith in him who suffered on the cross
we may triumph in the power of his victory;
through Jesus Christ your Son our Lord,
who is alive and reigns with you,
in the unity of the Holy Spirit,
one God, now and for ever.

| *Reflection by* **Graham James**

Psalms **40**, 125 *or* **37***
Jeremiah 23.9-32
John 12.12-19

Thursday 30 March

Jeremiah 23.9-32
'... even in my house I have found their wickedness' (v.11)

When Jeremiah complains that 'the land is full of adulterers', he is not thinking simply of the betrayal of the marriage bed (although there was probably plenty of adultery going on). It's the unfaithfulness of the people and their priests to God that's causing him distress. The worship of Baal with all its associated fertility rites is even found in the temple in Jerusalem – and with the sanction of Judah's religious leaders. What possessed them?

More than a century earlier, the Assyrian king Sennacherib laid siege to Jerusalem but failed to take it and retreated to his own land. The whole event was interpreted as proof that God always protected the temple, his dwelling place on earth. This conviction left a false sense of security. The people of Judah thought they were invincible because God would never let his temple be destroyed. So they partied and sinned, reckless of the consequences.

Nations and individuals may have almost unaccountable experiences of deliverance or liberation – from a threat or illness or some other enemy. The response may be one of gratitude leading to humility or an arrogance derived from a false superiority. Jeremiah hated the arrogance he saw around him. Think of the arrogance of superpowers today, or the conceit of those who think themselves protected by their wealth or power from adversity. By contrast, Jesus blesses the meek and humble of heart. Whom do we resemble?

Gracious Father,
you gave up your Son
out of love for the world:
lead us to ponder the mysteries of his passion,
that we may know eternal peace
through the shedding of our Saviour's blood,
Jesus Christ our Lord.

COLLECT

Reflection by **Graham James** | 39

Friday 31 March

Jeremiah 24

'I will give them a heart …' (v.7)

The heart is the organ of the body with the highest profile in the Bible, with 826 separate references according to a concordance on my bookshelves. Frequently, it is mentioned in conjunction with the mind, as in 'my heart and in my mind' (1 Samuel 2.35). According to the Bible, the heart is where the life force within us is found. It is definitely not merely a pump keeping the blood flowing within our bodies. From the heart flow good desires such as love, obedience and compassion. But the heart can deceive as well. It may generate pride, lust and hatred. 'We have followed too much the devices and desires of our own hearts', as the general confession in the Book of Common Prayer puts it. The metaphor of the heart as both the deepest source of inspiration and guidance as well as folly and deceit, is alive and well in our language today.

Jeremiah expects a renewed nation to be built following the people's exile in Babylon, but will unfaithfulness and disloyalty to God's law emerge in Israel again? The people seem to have been not just unwilling but unable to be obedient. So Jeremiah ponders God giving his people a new heart so that they will be so united with him that they will 'know that I am the Lord'. This will not be obedience through fear but through love. Something new is stirring here that Christians see fully revealed in Jesus Christ.

COLLECT

Most merciful God,
who by the death and resurrection of your Son Jesus Christ
delivered and saved the world:
grant that by faith in him who suffered on the cross
we may triumph in the power of his victory;
through Jesus Christ your Son our Lord,
who is alive and reigns with you,
in the unity of the Holy Spirit,
one God, now and for ever.

Reflection by **Graham James**

Psalms **23**, 127 *or* 41, **42**, 43
Jeremiah 25.1-14
John 12.36b-end

Saturday 1 April

Jeremiah 25.1-14

'King Nebuchadrezzar of Babylon, my servant ...' (v.9)

Through Jeremiah, the Lord is describing a pagan king, Nebuchadrezzar, as 'my servant'. Nebuchadrezzar (it's a variant spelling of Nebuchadnezzar but refers to the same person) is scarcely a model of propriety. Yet he is to be the agent used by the Lord to bring his people's waywardness to an end through defeat and exile, enabling a new opportunity to rebuild a more faithful nation.

Jewish tradition has long seen a later pagan king, Cyrus of Persia, as an agent of God too. He would conquer Babylon and allow the Jewish exiles to return. The idea of an unworthy person being God's agent has been alive in our own time. Some of President Trump's Christian supporters in the United States were well aware that he was scarcely a role model of Christian discipleship. They invoked the example of Cyrus (and could equally have cited Nebuchadrezzar) as someone God used for his good ends. In President Trump's case, they believed his opposition to abortion or his decision to recognize Jerusalem as the capital of Israel were among the things they believed were divinely guided.

The irony in Jeremiah describing Nebuchadrezzar as God's servant is that the king thought he was no-one's servant at all. He believed he was all-masterful. But his empire would be short-lived. Like many dictators or preening powerful people in the world today, his power was an illusion. He would have hated to be regarded as anyone's servant.

Gracious Father,
you gave up your Son
out of love for the world:
lead us to ponder the mysteries of his passion,
that we may know eternal peace
through the shedding of our Saviour's blood,
Jesus Christ our Lord.

COLLECT

Reflection by **Graham James** | 41

Monday 3 April
Monday of Holy Week

Psalm 41
Lamentations 1.1-12a
Luke 22.1-23

Luke 22.1-23

'Then Satan entered into Judas called Iscariot' (v.3)

Why do people do the things they do and, particularly, why do they do the awful things they do? The question of why people act in certain ways – especially when what they do has catastrophic consequences – is a question that is hard to avoid as we look around the world in which we live.

It is fascinating, therefore, to notice that the Gospel writers appeared to have asked the same question when they thought about Judas Iscariot – and even more interesting to observe that they seem to give different answers. Mark gives no answer, restricting himself to the simple account that Judas sought to betray Jesus to the chief priests (Mark 14.10). Matthew associates Judas' actions with greed – he asked what they would give him for betraying Jesus – but then reports his remorse and subsequent suicide (Matthew 26.14-16 and 27.3-10). John's Gospel declares it to be the devil who had 'put it into the heart of Judas son of Simon Iscariot to betray him' (John 13.2). Luke's explanation is closest to John's – Satan entered into Judas – but it doesn't go so far as to say it was all Satan's idea.

So why did Judas do what he did? Was it all down to the devil? Was it his own idea, driven by greed? Or are we better not to know why he acted as he did? We face the same questions as we look at the world today – why do people do what they do? As with Judas, we may never know the answer, but asking the question remains important.

C O L L E C T	Almighty and everlasting God, who in your tender love towards the human race sent your Son our Saviour Jesus Christ to take upon him our flesh and to suffer death upon the cross: grant that we may follow the example of his patience and humility, and also be made partakers of his resurrection; through Jesus Christ your Son our Lord, who is alive and reigns with you, in the unity of the Holy Spirit, one God, now and for ever.

42 | *Reflection by* **Paula Gooder**

Psalm 27
Lamentations 3.1-18
Luke 22. [24-38] 39-53

Tuesday 4 April
Tuesday of Holy Week

Luke 22. [24-38] 39-53

'Pray that you may not come into the time of trial' (v.40)

People often comment on the humanity of Jesus that is revealed in this passage. Here we see Jesus vulnerable, scared and suffering, begging his father to remove this cup from him.

It seems to me, however, that Jesus' own humanity is drawn into even sharper relief by another kind of humanity revealed in the actions of his companions. Jesus urges them to pray that they might not come into the time of trial, but instead they fall asleep, oblivious to the looming danger that is about to consume them and change their lives forever. Luke attempts to excuse the disciples on the grounds that they were worn out from grief (something not found in any of the other Gospels), but the contrast remains stark. Jesus, fully aware of what is about to befall him, turns to face it, even though he knows it will bring him untold suffering and pain. The disciples, unable to wrap their minds around the unfolding events, are overwhelmed and fall asleep.

Luke calls on us, the readers, to feel sympathy not just for Jesus, caught in the grip of horror at what was about to happen, but also for the disciples who are napping, completely unaware of what is about to befall them. By observing the grief of the one and the obliviousness of the other, we are drawn into the full tragedy of what is about to happen.

True and humble king,
hailed by the crowd as Messiah:
grant us the faith to know you and love you,
that we may be found beside you
on the way of the cross,
which is the path of glory.

COLLECT

Reflection by **Paula Gooder**   43

Wednesday 5 April
Wednesday of Holy Week

Psalm 102 [*or* 102.1-18]
Wisdom 1.16 – 2.1; 2.12-22
or Jeremiah 11.18-20
Luke 22.54-end

Luke 22.54-end

'The Lord turned and looked at Peter' (v.61)

Of all of the accounts of Peter's betrayal, Luke's tugs at the heart strings the most. In the other Gospels, after his arrest Jesus was held somewhere inside, while Peter remained outside. This meant that Peter's betrayal took place behind his back. In Luke's Gospel, Jesus is still in the courtyard while Peter denied him and, not only that, turned to look at him as the cock crowed. In other words, Peter denied Jesus almost to his face.

There is something profoundly powerful about this. Whether or not Luke's depiction of the scene is accurate, it packs a bigger emotional punch to have Peter deny Jesus in his presence. It challenges us to reflect on why Peter denied Jesus and, hence also, why we do unfathomable things of a similar nature.

Did Peter imagine that he could deny Jesus without Jesus knowing anything about it because he was elsewhere? Luke says no. Peter knew that Jesus would know that he had denied him and did it anyway. Perhaps he was driven by panic or maybe by anger? Perhaps the emotion of Jesus' arrest threw him off course temporarily? Perhaps his denial revealed something else of which Peter was previously unaware? It isn't even clear if Peter himself knew why he had denied Jesus – he just did. It is this to which Luke draws our attention in this simple phrase, 'The Lord turned and looked at Peter.'

COLLECT

Almighty and everlasting God,
who in your tender love towards the human race
    sent your Son our Saviour Jesus Christ
to take upon him our flesh
and to suffer death upon the cross:
grant that we may follow the example of his patience and humility,
and also be made partakers of his resurrection;
through Jesus Christ your Son our Lord,
who is alive and reigns with you,
in the unity of the Holy Spirit,
one God, now and for ever.

| *Reflection by* **Paula Gooder**

Psalms 42, 43
Leviticus 16.2-24
Luke 23.1-25

Thursday 6 April
Maundy Thursday

Luke 23.1-25

'... he sent him off to Herod' (v.7)

In the readings this week, I have been drawing attention to those parts of Luke's narrative that are uniquely Luke. Today's reading is no different.

Luke's Gospel is the only one that reports Jesus being sent to be tried by Herod. The Herod in question was Herod Antipas, son of Herod the Great, on whose death, Herod Antipas began to rule over Galilee and Perea in the north of the kingdom. He also had a palace in Jerusalem. Luke's account envisages that Jesus was sent to the ruler of his home region – Galilee – for a verdict when Pilate found it impossible to decide for himself.

The way that Luke presents his account of Jesus' trial suggests that Pilate was passing the buck. Faced with an impossible choice, of either killing a man he believed to be innocent or aggravating an angry mob, he passed the responsibility on. Herod, Luke notes, promptly passed it back again. The whole episode communicates a sense of profound discomfort and unease. Even Pilate, whose reputation for brutality was so well known that it eventually led to his removal from office, felt so uncomfortable that he tried to force someone else to make the decision for him. Imagine what would have happened if one of them had not dodged the difficult task but taken responsibility and declared Jesus to be as innocent as they knew him to be. Then as now, passing the buck may be tempting, but it never produces the right result.

> True and humble king,
> hailed by the crowd as Messiah:
> grant us the faith to know you and love you,
> that we may be found beside you
> on the way of the cross,
> which is the path of glory.

COLLECT

Friday 7 April
Good Friday

Psalm 69
Genesis 22.1-18
Hebrews 10.1-10

Hebrews 10.1-10

'I have come to do your will' (v.7)

The book of Hebrews can be incredibly hard to understand and this passage is no exception. One of the factors that make it so difficult is its mode of argument, which is very different from how we make a case today.

At the heart of this passage is the author's belief that Jesus is so much the fulfilment of Scripture, that quoting from a Psalm (here Psalm 40.7-9) is effectively quoting the words of Jesus. So the argument in this passage goes: sacrifice for sin was not effective because the priests had to keep on doing it (if it had been effective, sin would have been so wiped out that people no longer sinned). In any case, sacrifice was not what God wanted, as Psalm 40.7-8 makes clear. Christ came to do what God *did* want; in doing so, he abolished what was past and established a new way of being.

The very heart of this passage then is focused in this simple phrase: 'I have come to do your will.' Whatever our view of Hebrews' description of law and sacrifice, this is a beautiful summary of the nature of Christ and worth mulling on today of all days. Christ came to do the will of God and to show us what a life lived entirely focused on God's will can look like.

COLLECT

Almighty Father,
look with mercy on this your family
for which our Lord Jesus Christ was content to be betrayed
    and given up into the hands of sinners
    and to suffer death upon the cross;
who is alive and glorified with you and the Holy Spirit,
one God, now and for ever.

Reflection by **Paula Gooder**

Psalm 142
Hosea 6.1-6
John 2.18-22

Saturday 8 April
Easter Eve

John 2.18-22

'I will raise it up' (v.19)

I have always felt a certain sympathy for those who ask questions of the Jesus of John's Gospel. After his responses, it feels as though an awkward silence would fall as those who asked the question in the first place looked at each other trying to work out how on earth his answer related to their original question.

The reference to the temple being under construction for 46 years is a reference to Herod the Great's rebuilding of the second temple. The first iteration of the second temple, built after the exile, was completed in 515 BC but Herod began to expand and rebuild it in 20 BC. This rebuilding continued after his death and would potentially date this conversation, if the dates are correct, to AD 26.

No wonder the Jews were confused, but in the confusion lies a vital strand of Johannine theology. For Jews, the temple was the gateway to heaven, the place where, in the holy of holies, God could come to dwell among God's people and they could, on certain occasions, such as Isaiah's vision in Isaiah 6.1-10, see God seated on the throne in heaven. Jesus is saying here – as he does elsewhere in John – that he, the Word made flesh, was now the gateway to heaven. In him is direct access to God. In him God dwells among us, even as we await his resurrection in the darkness of Holy Saturday.

COLLECT

Grant, Lord,
that we who are baptized into the death
of your Son our Saviour Jesus Christ
may continually put to death our evil desires
and be buried with him;
and that through the grave and gate of death
we may pass to our joyful resurrection;
through his merits,
who died and was buried and rose again for us,
your Son Jesus Christ our Lord.

Reflection by **Paula Gooder**

47

Morning Prayer – a simple form

O Lord, open our lips
and our mouth shall proclaim your praise.

A prayer of thanksgiving for Lent *(for Passiontide see p. 50)*

Blessed are you, Lord God of our salvation,
to you be glory and praise for ever.
In the darkness of our sin you have shone in our hearts
to give the light of the knowledge of the glory of God
in the face of Jesus Christ.
Open our eyes to acknowledge your presence,
that freed from the misery of sin and shame
we may grow into your likeness from glory to glory.
Blessed be God, Father, Son and Holy Spirit.
Blessed be God for ever.

Word of God

Psalmody *(the psalm or psalms listed for the day)*

**Glory to the Father and to the Son
and to the Holy Spirit;
as it was in the beginning is now:
and shall be for ever. Amen.**

Reading from Holy Scripture *(one or both of the passages set for the day)*

Reflection

The Benedictus (The Song of Zechariah) *(see opposite page)*

Prayers

Intercessions – a time of prayer for the day and its tasks, the world and its need, the church and her life.

The Collect for the Day

The Lord's Prayer *(see p. 51)*

Conclusion

A blessing or the Grace *(see p. 51)*, or a concluding response

Let us bless the Lord
Thanks be to God

Benedictus (The Song of Zechariah)

1 Blessed be the Lord the God of Israel, ♦
    who has come to his people and set them free.

2 He has raised up for us a mighty Saviour, ♦
    born of the house of his servant David.

3 Through his holy prophets God promised of old ♦
    to save us from our enemies,
        from the hands of all that hate us,

4 To show mercy to our ancestors, ♦
    and to remember his holy covenant.

5 This was the oath God swore to our father Abraham: ♦
    to set us free from the hands of our enemies,

6 Free to worship him without fear, ♦
    holy and righteous in his sight
        all the days of our life.

7 And you, child, shall be called the prophet of the Most High, ♦
    for you will go before the Lord to prepare his way,

8 To give his people knowledge of salvation ♦
    by the forgiveness of all their sins.

9 In the tender compassion of our God ♦
    the dawn from on high shall break upon us,

10 To shine on those who dwell in darkness
        and the shadow of death, ♦
    and to guide our feet into the way of peace.

Luke 1.68-79

**Glory to the Father and to the Son
and to the Holy Spirit;
as it was in the beginning is now:
and shall be for ever. Amen.**

Seasonal Prayers of Thanksgiving

Passiontide

Blessed are you, Lord God of our salvation,
to you be praise and glory for ever.
As a man of sorrows and acquainted with grief
your only Son was lifted up
that he might draw the whole world to himself.
May we walk this day in the way of the cross
and always be ready to share its weight,
declaring your love for all the world.
Blessed be God, Father, Son and Holy Spirit.
Blessed be God for ever.

At Any Time

Blessed are you, creator of all,
to you be praise and glory for ever.
As your dawn renews the face of the earth
bringing light and life to all creation,
may we rejoice in this day you have made;
as we wake refreshed from the depths of sleep,
open our eyes to behold your presence
and strengthen our hands to do your will,
that the world may rejoice and give you praise.
Blessed be God, Father, Son and Holy Spirit.
Blessed be God for ever.

after Lancelot Andrewes (1626)

The Lord's Prayer and The Grace

Our Father in heaven,
hallowed be your name,
your kingdom come,
your will be done,
on earth as in heaven.
Give us today our daily bread.
Forgive us our sins
as we forgive those who sin against us.
Lead us not into temptation
but deliver us from evil.
For the kingdom, the power,
and the glory are yours
now and for ever.
Amen.

(or)

Our Father, who art in heaven,
hallowed be thy name;
thy kingdom come;
thy will be done;
on earth as it is in heaven.
Give us this day our daily bread.
And forgive us our trespasses,
as we forgive those who trespass against us.
And lead us not into temptation;
but deliver us from evil.
For thine is the kingdom,
the power and the glory,
for ever and ever.
Amen.

The grace of our Lord Jesus Christ,
and the love of God,
and the fellowship of the Holy Spirit,
be with us all evermore.
Amen.

An Order for Night Prayer (Compline)

The Lord almighty grant us a quiet night and a perfect end.
Amen.

Our help is in the name of the Lord
who made heaven and earth.

A period of silence for reflection on the past day may follow.

The following or other suitable words of penitence may be used

**Most merciful God,
we confess to you,
before the whole company of heaven and one another,
that we have sinned in thought, word and deed
and in what we have failed to do.
Forgive us our sins,
heal us by your Spirit
and raise us to new life in Christ. Amen.**

O God, make speed to save us.
O Lord, make haste to help us.

**Glory to the Father and to the Son
and to the Holy Spirit;
as it was in the beginning is now
and shall be for ever. Amen.
Alleluia.**

The following or another suitable hymn may be sung

Before the ending of the day,
Creator of the world, we pray
That you, with steadfast love, would keep
Your watch around us while we sleep.

From evil dreams defend our sight,
From fears and terrors of the night;
Tread underfoot our deadly foe
That we no sinful thought may know.

O Father, that we ask be done
Through Jesus Christ, your only Son;
And Holy Spirit, by whose breath
Our souls are raised to life from death.

The Word of God

Psalmody

One or more of Psalms 4, 91 or 134 may be used.

Psalm 134

1   Come, bless the Lord, all you servants of the Lord, ♦
      you that by night stand in the house of the Lord.

2   Lift up your hands towards the sanctuary ♦
      and bless the Lord.

3   The Lord who made heaven and earth ♦
      give you blessing out of Zion.

Glory to the Father and to the Son
and to the Holy Spirit;
as it was in the beginning is now
and shall be for ever. Amen.

Scripture Reading

One of the following short lessons or another suitable
passage is read

You, O Lord, are in the midst of us and we are called by your
name; leave us not, O Lord our God.

Jeremiah 14.9

(or)

Be sober, be vigilant, because your adversary the devil is
prowling round like a roaring lion, seeking for someone
to devour. Resist him, strong in the faith.

1 Peter 5.8,9

(or)

The servants of the Lamb shall see the face of God, whose name
will be on their foreheads. There will be no more night: they will
not need the light of a lamp or the light of the sun, for God will
be their light, and they will reign for ever and ever.

Revelation 22.4,5

Into your hands, O Lord, I commend my spirit.
Into your hands, O Lord, I commend my spirit.
For you have redeemed me, Lord God of truth.
I commend my spirit.
Glory to the Father and to the Son
and to the Holy Spirit.
Into your hands, O Lord, I commend my spirit.

Or, in Easter

Into your hands, O Lord, I commend my spirit.
    Alleluia, alleluia.
Into your hands, O Lord, I commend my spirit.
    Alleluia, alleluia.
For you have redeemed me, Lord God of truth.
Alleluia, alleluia.
Glory to the Father and to the Son
and to the Holy Spirit.
Into your hands, O Lord, I commend my spirit.
    Alleluia, alleluia.

Keep me as the apple of your eye.
Hide me under the shadow of your wings.

Gospel Canticle

Nunc Dimittis (The Song of Simeon)

**Save us, O Lord, while waking,
and guard us while sleeping,
that awake we may watch with Christ
and asleep may rest in peace.**

1   Now, Lord, you let your servant go in peace:
     your word has been fulfilled.

2   My own eyes have seen the salvation
     which you have prepared in the sight of every people;

3   A light to reveal you to the nations
     and the glory of your people Israel.

Luke 2.29-32

Glory to the Father and to the Son
and to the Holy Spirit;
as it was in the beginning is now
and shall be for ever. Amen.

Save us, O Lord, while waking,
and guard us while sleeping,
that awake we may watch with Christ
and asleep may rest in peace.

Prayers

Intercessions and thanksgivings may be offered here.

The Collect

Visit this place, O Lord, we pray,
and drive far from it the snares of the enemy;
may your holy angels dwell with us and guard us in peace,
and may your blessing be always upon us;
through Jesus Christ our Lord.
Amen.

The Lord's Prayer (see p. 51) may be said.

The Conclusion

In peace we will lie down and sleep;
for you alone, Lord, make us dwell in safety.

Abide with us, Lord Jesus,
for the night is at hand and the day is now past.

As the night watch looks for the morning,
so do we look for you, O Christ.

[Come with the dawning of the day
and make yourself known in the breaking of the bread.]

The Lord bless us and watch over us;
the Lord make his face shine upon us and be gracious to us;
the Lord look kindly on us and give us peace.
Amen.

Love what you've read?

Why not consider using
Reflections for Daily Prayer
all year round? We also
publish these meditations
on Bible readings in an
annual format, containing
material for the entire
Church year.

The volume for 2023/24
will be published in
May 2023 and features
contributions from a host
of distinguished writers:
Ally Barrett, John Barton,
Gregory Cameron, Andrew Davison,
Alan Everett, Peter Graystone, Malcolm Guite,
Colin Heber-Percy, Chine McDonald, Rachel Mann,
Anna Matthews, Nadim Nasser, Emma Parker,
David Runcorn, Jane Steen, Angela Tilby,
Margaret Whipp and Lucy Winkett. The reflections for
Holy Week 2024 are written by Stephen Cottrell.

Reflections for Daily Prayer:
Advent 2023 to the eve of Advent 2024

ISBN 978 1 78140 395 2
Available May 2023

REFLECTIONS FOR DAILY PRAYER
App

Make Bible study and reflection a part of your routine wherever you go with the Reflections for Daily Prayer App for Apple and Android devices.

Download the app for free from the App Store (Apple devices) or Google Play (Android devices) and receive a week's worth of reflections free. Then purchase a monthly, three-monthly or annual subscription to receive up-to-date content.

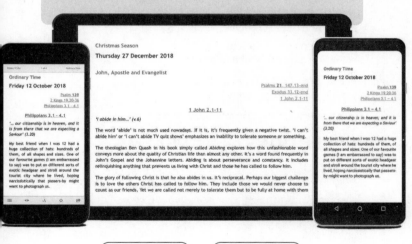

REFLECTIONS FOR SUNDAYS (YEAR A)

Reflections for Sundays offers over 250 reflections on the Principal Readings for every Sunday and major Holy Day in Year A, from the same experienced team of writers that have made *Reflections for Daily Prayer* so successful. For each Sunday and major Holy Day, they provide:

- full lectionary details for the Principal Service
- a reflection on each Old Testament reading (both Continuous and Related)
- a reflection on the Epistle
- a reflection on the Gospel.

£14.99 • 288 pages
ISBN 978 0 7151 4735 1

This book also contains a substantial introduction to the Gospel of Matthew, written by Paula Gooder.

Reflections for Sundays is also available in separate volumes for **Years B** *and* **C**.

Also available in Kindle and epub formats

REFLECTIONS ON THE PSALMS

£14.99 • 192 pages
ISBN 978 0 7151 4490 9

Reflections on the Psalms provides original and insightful meditations on each of the Bible's 150 Psalms.

Each reflection is accompanied by its corresponding Psalm refrain and prayer from the *Common Worship Psalter*, making this a valuable resource for personal or devotional use.

Specially written introductions by Paula Gooder and Steven Croft explore the Psalms and the Bible and the Psalms in the life of the Church.